Jewelry Making for Beginners

A Beginner's Guide to Designing Handmade Accessories

Flora Rodriguez

© Copyright 2024 - All rights reserved.

The contents of this book may not be reproduced, duplicated, or transmitted without the direct written permission of the author or publisher.

Under no circumstances will the publisher or author be held liable for any damages, recovery, or financial loss due to the information contained in this book. Neither directly nor indirectly.

Legal Notice:

This book is protected by copyright. This book is for personal use only. You may not modify, distribute, sell, use, quote, or paraphrase any part or content of this book without the permission of the author or publisher.

Disclaimer Notice:

Please note that the information contained in this document is for educational and entertainment purposes only. Every effort has been made to present accurate, current, reliable, and complete information. No warranties of any kind are stated or implied. The reader acknowledges that the author is not offering legal, financial, medical, or professional advice. The contents of this book have been taken from various sources. Please consult a licensed professional before attempting any of the techniques described in this book.

By reading this document, the reader agrees that under no circumstances will the author be liable for any direct or indirect loss arising from the use of the information contained in this document, including but not limited to - errors, omissions, or inaccuracies.

Table of Contents

Introduction 4
Chapter 1: Your Essentials Tools. 6
Chapter 2: The Basic Techniques. 23
Chapter 3: Design Your Own Bead Jewelry. 36
Chapter 4: Bead Stringing & Knotting. 45
Chapter 5: Wire Wrapping. 60
Chapter 6: Craft Your Jewels. 74
Conclusion 118

Introduction

Imagine wearing a piece of jewelry that's not just stylish, but entirely your own creation—designed by you, for you. Whether it's a pair of elegant earrings, a bold statement necklace, or a delicate bracelet, making your own jewelry unlocks a world of creativity and personal expression.

In this book, you'll discover how easy and enjoyable it can be to turn your ideas into stunning pieces, even if you've never crafted a thing in your life. From selecting the right tools and materials to mastering simple techniques, you'll be able to create beautiful, wearable art in no time.

Whether you're looking for a new hobby, a way to express yourself, or even a path to starting your own jewelry business, this beginner's guide is your perfect starting point.

As you go through these pages, you'll discover how to choose the best materials, become an expert in fundamental skills, and gain an understanding of design ideas that can turn commonplace parts into exceptional ones. Beyond the specifics, though, you'll experience the pleasure of losing yourself in a contemplative process that not only results in stunning jewelry but also provides a break from the stress of daily life.

Therefore, "Jewelry Making for Beginners" will be your constant companion whether you're here to learn a new pastime, make thoughtful gifts, or even build the foundation for a possible business. As we set off on this glittering trip together, we invite you to let your creativity soar, your imagination soar, and your fingers dance through beads, wire, and stones.

Get ready to transform everyday materials into something extraordinary—and wear your creativity proudly!

Chapter 1: Your Essentials Tools.

When you first start making jewelry, it's crucial to become acquainted with the basic supplies you'll need to realize your artistic goals. The purpose of these instruments is to improve the process's efficiency, enjoyment, and smoothness. Let's examine each tool and how well it fits different jewelry-making tasks:

1. **Chain-Nose Pliers:** The tapered, pointed jaws of chain-nose pliers make them an extremely useful instrument. They work great for holding, bending, and gripping small parts like wire, beads, and jump rings. You can precisely bend them and work in confined locations because to their compact form. When performing activities that call for control and precision, these pliers are an absolute need.

2. **Round-Nose Pliers:** The rounded, conical jaws of these pliers are ideal for shaping wire into coils, loops, and curves. They're perfect for crafting delicate wirework,

jump rings, and earring hooks. Your jewelry creations will look more polished thanks to the tapered jaws that let you make uniform loops in a range of sizes.

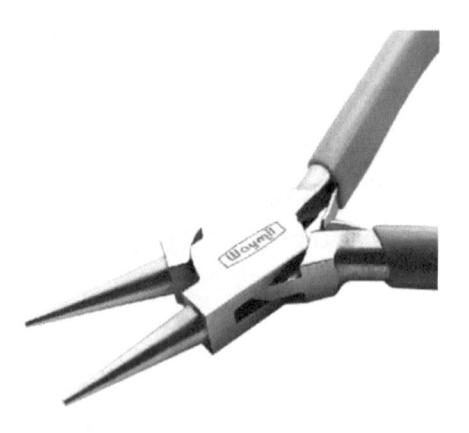

3. **Flat-Nose Pliers:** Flat-nose pliers have flat, smooth jaws that provide a strong grip without leaving marks on your materials. They're great for straightening wire, holding components, and making angular bends. These pliers come in handy when you need to manipulate and shape flat surfaces without causing damage.

4. **Wire Cutters:** Wire cutters are designed to cleanly and efficiently cut through different gauges of wire. They have sharp blades that create clean edges, preventing frayed ends on your wire. Whether you're snipping headpins, eye pins, or excess wire, wire cutters are indispensable for creating neat and professional-looking jewelry.

5. **Crimping Pliers:** Crimping pliers are essential for attaching clasps and securing crimp beads or tubes onto jewelry wire. They have notches that allow you to flatten crimps into secure closures, ensuring your pieces are durable and well-finished. Crimping pliers provide a polished and reliable way to fasten your designs.

6. **Beading Mat:** A beading mat provides a soft, non-slip surface where you can arrange and organize your beads, findings, and components. It prevents items from rolling away and keeps your workspace tidy. Beading mats are especially useful for preventing beads from rolling off your table while you work.

7. **Bead Scoop or Tweezers:** These tools are helpful for picking up and handling tiny beads, especially seed beads or smaller sized gemstones. A bead scoop has a small scoop-like end that allows you to gather beads efficiently, while tweezers can easily provide more precise control for placing individual beads exactly where you want them.

8. **Bead Design Board:** A bead design board is a useful tool for planning out your jewelry designs. It often features grooves and compartments where you can arrange beads and components to visualize the layout before stringing them together.

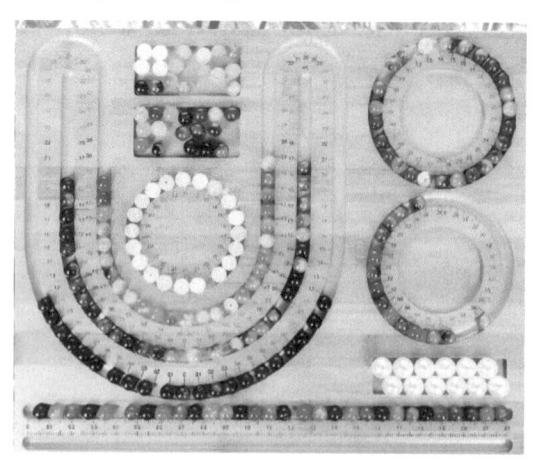

9. **Measuring Tools:** Having a ruler or a pair of calipers can be essential for measuring and cutting materials accurately. This is crucial for achieving balanced designs and ensuring your jewelry pieces are consistent in size.

10. **Bead Crimper Tool (Optional):** If you plan to work with multi-strand designs, a bead crimper tool can help you create neat and secure connections between strands and clasps.

Jewelry Making Materials You Will Need

1. Jewelry beads

In essence, beads are lovely items composed of various materials such as plastic, glass, metal, stone, wood, and precious materials. They serve as the foundation for your jewelry project since they may be used to build a wide range of jewelry designs, such as pendants, rings, bracelets, necklaces, and rings. They are composed of a material that has a hole in it to hold the beads in the jewelry.

There are many various kinds of beads available, so make sure you select the one that best suits your tastes.

Types of Jewelry Beads

They are available in a broad range of materials, forms, sizes, and finishes, which give the designs more texture, color, and visual interest. The following are explanations of many bead kinds that are frequently used in jewelry making:

- Seed Beads: Glass or plastic seed beads are tiny, consistently formed beads. They were given this name because they are little and resemble seeds. Seed beads come in a range of sizes, from 15/0 (the smallest) to 6/0. (largest). Their beautiful weaving, embroidery, and beaded creations are well-known.

- Glass Beads: Because glass beads are formed of molten glass, they have a smooth, sparkling appearance. They come in a wide variety of forms, such as teardrop, bicone, oval, round, and faceted. The various colors, textures, and patterns of glass beads include transparent, opaque, frosted, iridescent, and dichroic.

- Gemstone Beads: Semi-precious stones and natural minerals are utilized to make gemstone beads. They have unique colors, designs, and characteristics. Popular gemstone beads include amethyst, turquoise, lapis lazuli, agate, jade, and jasper, among many others. Beads made of gemstones lend jewelry creations an air of sophistication and natural beauty.

- Crystal Beads: Precision-cut glass beads with a high lead content are called crystal beads because of their extraordinary clarity and brilliance. Due to their low cost, they are frequently used as gemstone bead substitutes. Numerous types of Swarovski crystals, including bicone, round, and teardrop shapes, are utilized in jewelry creation and are known for their high quality.

- Pearl Beads: Mollusks produce pearl beads when an irritant, such as a sand grain, enters their shell. They stand out for having glossy and smooth surfaces. Pearls can be either freshwater or saltwater, and they come in a variety of designs, including coins, coins, round, oval, and baroque pearls. They elevate and lend sophistication to jewelry creations.

- Metal Beads: Different metals, including brass, copper, sterling silver, gold-filled, and pewter, are used to make metal beads. They might be smooth, hammered, textured, filigree, or etched, among other finishes. Metal beads are adaptable and frequently utilized as focal points or spacers in jewelry designs.

- Wood Beads: Wood beads are thin and have an organic, natural appearance. They may be left unadorned or decorated in a variety of colors, patterns, or carvings. Designs for earthy, tribal, and bohemian jewelry frequently feature wood beads.

- Ceramic Beads: Ceramic beads come in a variety of forms, hues, and finishes and are produced from baked clay. They may be painted, glazed, or left unglazed for a more natural look. Jewelry designs benefit from the handmade and creative addition of ceramic beads.

- Acrylic Beads: Alternatives to glass beads that are lightweight and less expensive are acrylic beads. They come in a variety of forms, dimensions, and hues. Acrylic beads are adaptable for various jewelry styles since they may mimic the appearance of glass, gemstones, pearls, and other materials.

2. Wire and Stringing Materials:

➢ **Beading Wire:** Beading wire is a flexible and versatile stringing material that's widely used in jewelry making. It's typically composed of multiple strands of stainless steel wire coated with nylon or other materials to prevent kinks and increase durability. Beading wire comes in different thicknesses, or gauges, and can be classified by the number of strands it contains. Common gauges include 0.015", 0.018", and 0.024".

- Beading wire is strong, flexible, and suitable for jewelry designs. It's commonly used for necklaces, bracelets, and anklets, especially for heavier beads. Choose the right gauge based on weight and desired flexibility, with thinner gauges offering more flexibility.

➢ **Tiger Tail Wire:** Tiger Tail is a stiff, stainless steel wire that's coated with nylon. It's known for its rigidity and strength, which makes it ideal for projects that require structure and stability.

- Tiger Tail wire is a sturdy, flexible nylon coating suitable for creating necklaces and bracelets with larger beads, crystals, and gemstones, but may be challenging for intricate or delicate designs due to its stiffness.

➢ **Stretch Cord:** Stretch cord is a type of elastic cord that allows you to create bracelets without the need for clasps. It's easy to use and provides a comfortable fit.

- Stretch cord, elastic and pre-strung with beads, is commonly used for creating beaded bracelets and children's jewelry. However, it can lose elasticity over time, so it's crucial to use quality cord with slack.

➢ **Leather Cord:** Leather cord adds a rustic and natural look to jewelry designs. It comes in various thicknesses and colors.

- Leather cord, a flexible, unique texture, is popular for creating bohemian or casual jewelry, often used in necklaces, bracelets, and anklets. It pairs well with natural materials, but requires appropriate findings and fastenings.

➢ **Silk Thread:** Silk thread is a delicate stringing material that's often used for creating elegant and traditional-style jewelry. It's typically used for stringing pearls and other delicate beads.

- Silk thread, soft and supple, is used for stringing delicate beads, adding sophistication to jewelry. Despite its less durable nature, it's popular for bridal and formal jewelry. Careful handling and knotting are essential.

3. **Findings:**

Findings are essential components in jewelry making, connecting and finishing pieces, providing functionality and aesthetic value. Common types include wire, beads, and crystals.

- **Clasps:** Clasps are closures that secure bracelets, necklaces, and anklets. They come in various styles, each with its own mechanism for opening and closing. Some popular types of clasps include:

    - **Lobster Clasp:** A spring-loaded clasp that opens when you push down on the small lever and closes when released.

    - **Toggle Clasp:** A two-piece clasp consisting of a bar that goes through a circular or "T" shaped loop to secure the piece.

    - **Magnetic Clasp:** A clasp with magnets that attract and hold the pieces together. It's easy to use but might not be suitable for heavy pieces.

- **Jump Rings:** Jump rings are small, circular rings that are often used to connect components. They can be used to attach clasps, pendants, charms, and more. Jump rings come in different sizes and gauges, and they can be opened using pliers for attaching or detaching components.

- ➢ **Ear Wires:** Ear wires, also known as ear hooks or earwires, are used to create earrings. They come in various designs, including simple hooks, kidney wires, and lever-backs. The open loop at the bottom allows you to attach your earring designs.

- ➢ **Headpins and Eyepins:** Headpins have a flat or decorative end (the "head") and a straight wire that can be used to dangle beads or create drops. Eyepins have a loop at one end and are used to create beaded links or dangles.

- ➢ **Crimp Beads and Tubes:** Crimp beads and tubes are used to secure the ends of beading wire. They are flattened using crimping pliers to create a secure connection that prevents beads from sliding off. Crimps are often used with clasps and other findings.

➢ **Bail:** A bail is a component that's attached to a pendant to allow it to hang from a chain or cord. Bails come in various shapes, sizes, and styles, such as pinch bails, glue-on bails, and fold-over bails.

➢ **Spacer Beads:** Spacer beads are small beads used to separate and add visual interest between larger beads. They can be simple metal beads or decorative accents that complement your design.

➢ **End Caps:** End caps are used to finish the ends of cords or multiple strands of beading wire. They provide a polished look and can also provide a connection point for clasps.

- **Crimp Covers:** Crimp covers are small, hollow metal beads used to hide crimped connections, creating a more professional and polished appearance.

- **Split Rings:** Similar to jump rings, split rings are used to attach charms or small pendants. They are more secure than regular jump rings and are often used for keychains and pieces that may experience more wear.

- **Connectors and Links:** Connectors and links are decorative findings that can be used to join different elements in your jewelry. They often feature intricate designs, and they can be used to create chain necklaces, bracelets, and more.

4. **Pendants and Charms:**

Pendants, decorative elements in jewelry, come in various shapes, sizes, and materials. They can be simple or intricate and can represent personal interests, passions, or sentimental values. Common styles include lockets, cameos, gemstone pendants, and bezel-set crystals.

Chapter 2: The Basic Techniques.

1. Opening Jump Rings

Mastering the technique of opening jump rings is crucial in bead jewelry making, enabling the connection of components and attachment of charms, pendants, and clasps. Here's a step-by-step guide on how to properly open jump rings for your bead jewelry projects:

Materials Needed:

- Jump rings
- Chain-nose pliers
- Flat-nose pliers (optional, for extra stability)
- Charms, pendants, or other components
- Jewelry findings (clasps, ear wires, etc.)

Steps:

1. **Gather Your Materials:** Ensure you have all your jump rings, components, and pliers ready on your workspace.

2. **Choose the Right Pliers:** Chain-nose pliers are the primary tool for opening jump rings. They have a tapered, flat surface that provides a good grip. If you're new to this technique, you might find flat-nose pliers helpful as they provide more stability.

3. **Hold the Jump Ring:** Use the chain-nose pliers to firmly grasp the jump ring on either side of the cut. Ensure the cut is facing you and the opening is at the top.

4. **Twist, Don't Pull:** Instead of pulling the jump ring apart, gently twist one end away from you while keeping the other end steady. This twisting motion helps maintain the round shape of the jump ring.

5. **Add Components:** Slide your charm, pendant, or other component onto the jump ring. Ensure that it's centered and positioned as desired.

6. Close the Jump RingReverse the twisting motion by bringing the ends back together to shut the jump ring. Ensure there are no gaps or misalignments in the cut edges by aligning them.

7. **Check for a Secure Closure:** Run your fingertip along the jump ring's seam to ensure it's closed properly. The cut edges should meet seamlessly without any gaps.

8. **Use Flat-Nose Pliers (Optional):** If the jump ring isn't closing smoothly, you can gently squeeze the sides using flat-nose pliers. Be cautious not to deform the shape.

9. **Repeat as Needed:** Practice opening and closing jump rings until you're comfortable and achieve consistent results.

Tips and Considerations:

- Choose the right size for your project, avoid over opening, twist, and don't pull the ends. Practice makes perfect; use less expensive materials and secure closures to create strong connections in jewelry pieces. Combining jump rings with other techniques like wire wrapping or stringing can create complex designs.

2. Crimping

Crimping is a crucial technique in bead jewelry making, ensuring secure attachment of clasps, closures, and other components to beading wire, ensuring durability and professionalism. Here's a step-by-step guide on how to crimp beads in your bead jewelry projects:

Materials Needed:

- Beads or components
- Beading wire
- Crimp beads or tubes
- Crimping pliers
- Clasps or closures

Steps:

1. **Thread the Wire:** Slide the desired beads or components onto the beading wire, leaving an extra inch or two at the end for attaching the clasp.

2. **Add a Crimp Bead:** Slide a crimp bead or tube onto the wire. Ensure it's positioned close to the last bead but with a bit of space to allow movement.

3. Loop Through Clasp: Thread the wire end through the clasp's or closure's loop. After that, re-enter the wire via the crimp bead. Now that the clasp loop should be secure, the beading wire and crimp bead should have formed a loop.

4. Position and Flatten: Place the crimp bead 1/8 inch away from the clasp loop using your fingertips. This guarantees that there is adequate room to move without being excessively loose.

5. Chain-nose or flat-nose pliers are used to secure the crimp bead in place. Make sure the crimp bead is positioned in the larger depression (closer to the handle) of the crimping pliers, which is located over the bead.

6. **First Crimp:** Gently squeeze the crimping pliers to create a U-shape crimp in the crimp bead. This helps secure the bead onto the wire.

7. **Rotate the Bead:** Turn the crimp bead 90 degrees to the side. Position the crimping pliers over the bead, placing the crimp in the smaller indentation (closer to the tip) of the pliers.

8. **Second Crimp:** Squeeze the crimping pliers more firmly this time to create a rounded shape in the crimp bead. This completes the crimp and secures the wire.

9. **Trim Excess Wire:** Use wire cutters to trim the excess wire, leaving a short tail. Be careful not to cut the beading wire accidentally.

Tips and Considerations:

- Crimping pliers are essential for secure crimps while choosing the right crimps that match the wire's diameter is crucial. Avoid over crimping to avoid damage. Practice on a spare wire before finalizing. Ensure consistency in size and shape for a polished look. Test the crimp by gently tugging on the wire to ensure it's secure.

3. Tying Basic Knots

Tying knots is a crucial technique in bead jewelry making, securing components, spacing beads, and creating adjustable closures, essential for creating sturdy and visually appealing pieces. Here's a step-by-step guide on how to tie some common knots used in bead jewelry making:

Materials Needed:

- Beads or components
- Stringing material (beading wire, cord, leather, etc.)
- Clasp and findings (if needed)

Basic Knots:

1. **Overhand Knot:** One of the simplest knots, the overhand knot is frequently used to make a stopper or to add space between beads.

Steps:

1. Your beads should be strung up on the stringing material.
2. Create a loop with the stringing material, then tie an overhand knot in it.
3. The stringing material's end should be threaded through the loop.
4. Pull both ends of the stringing material to tighten the knot.

2. **Square Knot:** The square knot is used for creating adjustable closures and adding decorative elements to your jewelry pieces.

Steps:

1. Left string and right string are crossed.
2. The right string should be passed beneath the left string.
3. Raise and cross the right string over the left string.
4. Loop the right string through the left string's opening.

5. Pulling both strings in different directions will help you tighten the knot.

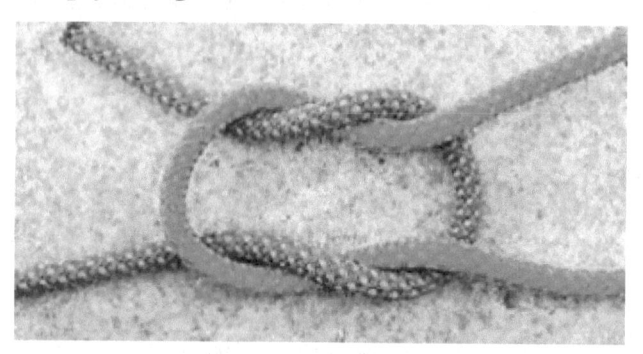

3. **Slip Knot:** Slip knots are used to make bracelets and necklaces with adjustable closures that are simple to put on and take off.

Steps:

1. Holding the stringing material between your thumb and forefinger, make a little loop.

2. The stringing material's end should be threaded through the loop.

3. Gently draw the loose ends to tighten the loop, forming a knot that can be adjusted.

4. **Lark's Head Knot:** The lark's head knot is used to attach pendants, charms, and other components to cords or chains.

Steps:

1. To make a loop, fold the stringing material in half.
2. Put the loop underneath the object to which you want to attach it.
3. The stringing material's loose ends should be inserted into the loop and pulled snugly.

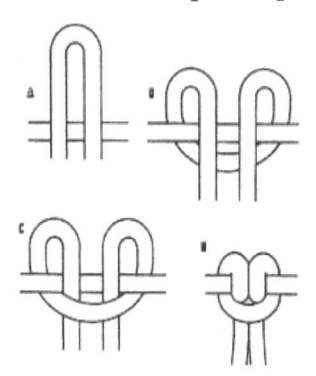

Tips and Considerations:

- Practice knots on spare stringing material before finalizing your piece. Choose the right knot for the job, maintain consistency in size and tightness, and choose appropriate stringing material. Test the knots by gently pulling the material to ensure secure holding. Leave enough space between beads for movement.

4. Forming A Simple Loop

Forming a simple loop is a fundamental technique in bead jewelry making that allows you to create secure and elegant connections for attaching beads, charms, pendants, and other components to chains, ear wires, and more. Mastering this technique is essential for creating well-crafted jewelry pieces with a professional finish. Here's a step-by-step guide on how to form a simple loop in your bead jewelry projects:

Materials Needed:

- Beads or components
- Wire (headpins or eyepins)
- Round-nose pliers
- Chain-nose pliers

Steps:

1. **Thread the Bead:** Slide the bead onto the headpin or eyepin, leaving some space at the top.

2. **Positioning the Bead:** Hold the wire just above the bead using chain-nose pliers. Ensure there's enough space between the bead and the pliers to create the loop.

3. **Create the Bend:** With the chain-nose pliers, bend the wire sharply at a 90-degree angle away from the bead. The bend should be close to the bead but not touching it.

4. **Positioning the Round-Nose Pliers:** Hold the wire with the round-nose pliers, gripping it at the point where the wire was bent. The bent portion should be positioned at the very edge of the pliers' jaws.

5. **Create the Loop:** Rotate your wrist slowly while maintaining a firm grip on the pliers to bring the end of the wire over the top jaw. The loop will begin to form as a result.

6. **Complete the Loop:** Continue rotating your wrist until the wire crosses over itself and forms a complete loop around the pliers. Ensure the loop is centered and symmetrical.

7. **Adjust the Loop:** If the loop is too tight or not perfectly round, you can use the round-nose pliers to gently adjust its shape.

8. **Trim Excess Wire:** You'll have a tail of wire sticking out from the loop after creating it. Trim the extra wire with wire cutters, leaving a short tail.

Tips and Considerations:

- Forming loops requires choosing appropriate wire, practicing, and aiming for consistency. Use round-nose or chain-nose pliers for round loops and pliers for gripping wire. For earrings, formed loops are commonly used. Experiment with different sizes by positioning round-nose pliers closer or farther from the bead.

5. Forming A Wrapped Beaded Loop

Forming a wrapped beaded loop is a sophisticated technique in bead jewelry making, ensuring secure and decorative connections for attaching beads, charms, pendants, and other components to chains, ear wires, and other components, adding an elegant touch.

Materials Needed:

- Beads or components
- Headpins or eyepins
- Wire (matching or contrasting color)
- Round-nose pliers
- Chain-nose pliers
- Wire cutters

Steps:

1. Bead Threading: Leave a gap at the top of the headpin or eyepin before sliding the bead onto it.

2. Making the Bend: The wire should be bent firmly at a 90-degree angle away from the bead using chain-nose

pliers. Although it shouldn't touch the bead, the bend should be near to it.

3. Setting the Round-Nose Pliers in Place: Using the round-nose pliers, hold the wire and grasp it where it was bent. The bent piece needs to be placed right on the pliers' jaw edges.

4. To make the loop, gently rotate your wrist while maintaining a firm grip on the pliers. This will bring the wire's end over the top jaw of the pliers. Similar to a simple loop, this will cause the loop to begin to form.

5. Begin Creating the loop: Hold the loop firmly in place with the round-nose pliers while positioning the wire's end against the stem with your free hand (wire below the bead).

6. Wrap the Wire: With your free hand, begin wrapping the wire around the stem beneath the loop by using your fingers or a pair of chain-nose pliers. The loop will be fixed in place after this.

7. Wrap the wire around the stem 2–3 times, depending on the thickness of the wire and the desired appearance.

8. Snip Extra Wire: After wrapping the wire around the stem a few times, trim any extra wire with wire cutters. Trim as closely as you can to the stem.

9. Tuck the End: Gently press and tuck the wire's cut end against the stem using chain-nose pliers. This keeps any pointy ends from protruding.

Tips and Considerations:

- Choose the right wire for wrapping beaded loops, ensuring it complements your design. Practice and patience are essential, as forming wrapped loops can be challenging. Ensure consistency and choose a wire gauge that matches component thickness. Wrapped beaded loops are commonly used in earrings and can be experimented with different patterns.

NOTE: We do understand that some of these techniques may be difficult for some unfamiliar with them to truly discern. We would like to suggest that if that is the case, please search that particular technique on YouTube, for a video tutorial, as we are of course unable to show video content here.

Chapter 3: Design Your Own Bead Jewelry.

1. How to Make Unique Earrings

Before making earrings, consider choosing metals like gold, copper, brass, aluminum, silver, nickel, or surgical steel for your jewelry brand. If customers are allergic, use titanium, plastic, nylon, or niobium. Choose earring gauges that fit comfortably, and carefully tumble or file tips to remove sharp edges. Plan flush cuts, reliable loops, and smooth ring closure. Use earring stoppers to prevent ear slipping. Use terminology like temper and makeup to identify wire properties, such as half-hard, soft, or hard.

How to get started

- The first stage entails purchasing the necessary supplies, such as gemstones, beads, headpins, and equipment like pliers, wire cutters, or design templates. It's crucial that you practice on less expensive materials as a beginner before moving on to more expensive materials like precious metals or rare jewels.

- The beads should be made of both commercially produced glass beads and semi-precious stones and minerals. Other affordable water pearls, while in smaller amounts, should be added to your design to make it more distinctive.

- Look for a bundle that contains pre-made ear wires when purchasing the headpins. These are less expensive than gold or silver and can help you learn a variety of skills. The pins or wires need to be long enough, ideally 1.5 to 2 inches.

- To make loops and curves, look for instruments like rosary pliers, which combine side-cutting with round-tip cutting.

- Before beginning difficult designs, start by crafting simple designs like bead earrings. If the wire you're using doesn't have a jump ring and is straight, you'll need to choose which side goes in the ear while making sure the long side is gently curled away.

- Make sure that the earrings' findings—such as screws or clips—are solid and functional in order to give the final design stability. Make sure your client's earrings are balanced, clean, and comfortable throughout the entire set.

- Instead of purchasing pre-made ear wires, you can save money by bending straightforward jewelry shapes. To create a distinctive brand that appeals to your customers, you must experiment with several styles.

To make a bead earring, this procedure serves as the basic tutorial to follow:

Find a headpin.

An ordinary pin with a rounded head or a flat bottom is referred to as a headpin. Different sizes and gauges are available (thickness). You can choose your chosen metal from the ones mentioned above because headpins come in a variety of metals.

Add your beads.

Put a spacer bead at the bottom of your soft, hard, or half-hard headpin before continuing. Continue with additional beads, making sure to use a variety of designs or hues. Separating the various colors is another usage for spacer beads. Just keep adding beads until there is just 6 to 10 mm between them and the headpin. You can use the wire cutters to cut your headpin to the desired length to create shorter earrings.

Bending the headpin

With a set of round-nose pliers, you can begin by bending your head-top pin's 90 degrees. Then, bend the top of the headpin to create a loop, allowing you to attach a wire to the end of the headpin to finish the earring. Make a clean loop using the pliers' tip as a guide starting from the headpin's end.

Completing the earrings

Add a French wire before you finish closing the earring finding or the loop post, and then follow the above instructions to make another pair of your original earrings.

If headpins are not an option, you can use plain wire pieces instead. To prevent your beads from falling off, make a loop from one side of the wire. You should finish off the loop or spiral just like a headpin. But select the cables that are advised, especially for the sections that go into the ears.

Depending on the thickness of your headpin, make sure you leave adequate room at the end. For a 24-gauge headpin, you need an allowance of about ¼ inch (6mm) but for a thicker headpin say gauge 18, you need to allow more room.

2. How to Make Rings

As a component of your jewelry collection, you can easily create your own distinctive rings. Simply take the following actions to create your design:

Determine how much money you'll need.

To buy the setting, gemstones, diamonds, and other necessities, you need a beginning budget of, say, $400. After that, choose the center stone you want, such as a sapphire, diamond, emerald, or ruby, taking your desired form and size into account.

Look for the environment.

There are various settings to consider, including three-stone, solitaire, and multi-stone configurations. Prepare to safely set the stones in your ring after creating it. To ensure it meets excellent quality standards, you must polish, clean, and then do a triple check.

How to Estimate a Ring's Size

A ring must be accurately sized to fit snugly and be big enough to go over the second knuckle. Since fingers are often smaller in the morning, measure your fingers at the end of the day. There are easy ways to measure the size of your finger, including using a thread, a ruler, and calipers. Other strategies include:

Remove the ring sizer.

This is the simplest way to get the several paper ring sizers that are accessible online for printing. All you have to do to take the measurement is wrap the paper band around your finger. Even better, you can cut a slit in a piece of paper, wear the resulting piece as binding for a belt.

Size of Ring Template

The other approach is to acquire a printed template with various ring diameters. Based on the worldwide ring sizing tables, this printable design really shows the exact diameter of the rings specified in millimeters. Individual rings are also applicable when the diameter is measured with a ruler.

3. How to Make Unique Necklaces

Stone or glass beads, which are readily available locally, can be used to create necklaces. You may construct a basic bead necklace by following the step-by-step instructions below.

1. Gather all of the supplies you require, such as beading threads and wires. The best wire to use is one that has 19, 21, or 49 strands of nylon-polished stainless-steel wire. You can use beading thread, which comes in a range of colors, to string lightweight beads. Get a silk cord that comes in a variety of colors and gauges.

2. Prior to cutting the wire or thread you're using for your necklace, determine its real length. For the connection to the clasp and other stringing materials, allow an extra 4 to 8 inches.

3. Depending on the style of necklace you want, collect the beads, 2 crimp beads, and 1 clasp. Simply place a tiny bead onto the treading material, and then crimp the head. After about one inch, add another tiny bead.

After the crimp bead, attach one end of the jump ring, which is also known as the clasp. Together with the stringing material, this will create a loop.

4. Simply insert the end of the stringing material through the clasp part, followed by the bead-crimp-bead combination. The beads can then be crimped into position using the chain nose pliers or another crimping tool. By taking these precautions, you can reduce the risk that the necklace will break due to the stringing materials rubbing against the ends of the crimp beads.

5. Before stringing, choose the beads you'll need to create your custom design. Before stringing, you can measure and plan out your design on a beading board. Now attach the beads to the

necklace as you had intended, leaving 3 to 4 inches of stringing material at the end.

Use a jump ring or clasp section, the bead-crimp-bead combination, and the remaining stringing material to press it into the bead holes up to the level of the crimp bead.

6. Be careful not to draw the stringing material too tightly; instead, leave a tiny margin of around 14 inches. Allowing the beads to freely rotate or move can prevent them from rubbing against one another. In contrast to the gently rounded necklace, a hard design appears sharp.

7. Crimp the opposite end last, and then use slush cutters to cut the leftover stringing material. Allow roughly 1 inch of wire when cutting the material but avoid cutting it too close to the crimp head. The necklace can freely stretch without breaking thanks to this tolerance.

4. How to Make Bracelets

Mastering basic skills like making friendship bracelets is a straightforward process. Gather materials like multicolored embroidery thread strands for distinctive patterns. Choose thick or narrow bracelets based on the required number of threads for an appealing design.

Cut the first strand after measuring it out.

Before you cut it, be sure the length you measured is indeed longer than the space between your shoulder and your fingertip. As a result, when the bracelet is worn around the wrist, it has room to expand. Measure and cut the additional strands from this cut thread to have a matching length and an allowance.

-Knot and secure the strands with pins.

Make a knot out of the strands, then pin them to a flat surface. As an alternative, you might use it to knot around your toe as a fun approach to finish the task. As opposed to using tape, firmly hold your bracelet in place by using the pinning method.

-Extend the threads widely.

To make the colors appear on the bracelet in the desired order, you need spread out your threads. To avoid making the bracelet's knotted end bulky, do not cross the threads too many times over one another.

Consider making a few little braids in your bracelet before beginning the pattern. Just like you would braid your hair or a three-strand bracelet, create three distinct strands and braid them together.

To secure the thread coming from the extreme left around the thread that is directly to its right, tie a "half-hitch" knot. The second pink thread can be covered with the green thread. Pull the first thread around the second, making sure to leave a loop to the left.

The first thread should be passed through the loop you just made. The knot should rise to the top of the second thread as you pull it up. The thread being used to tie the knot needs to be held firmly in place and positioned correctly.

Now, working from left to right, knot the thread on the far left around the remaining threads. Using the green thread, tie another "half hitch" knot around each of the other strands in a corresponding direction (left to right). Just tie two of the same knots on each thread before continuing. The green thread should be travelling all the way to the far right at the finish.

-Make sure that each thread ends up on the right side by knotting it to the thread that is farthest to the left for the remaining threads from left to right.

Start each time with a single color of thread, unless you want to combine two threads of the same color. Make the bracelet longer by knotting it in accordance with the wrist it is intended to suit. Test first on your own wrist, leaving roughly 2 fingers of room after fitting.

-Now, if desired, braid the ends of the bracelet using as many braids as you did at the beginning.

The strands can be embellished with charms or tiny beads before being knotted together to give them stability. Trim the extra thread off the bracelet's opposite end with scissors once you've tied a knot in it.

Once you've tied both ends of your bracelet together, tighten it up by tying another knot if necessary.

Chapter 4: Bead Stringing & Knotting.

Bead stringing and knotting are crucial jewelry making techniques, enabling artisans to create stunning, personalized pieces by threading beads onto stringing material and strategically placing knots for spacing and closures.

The Bead Stringing and Knotting Process:

Bead Selection and Design: The journey begins with selecting the beads that will form the heart of your design. Beads come in various shapes, sizes, colors, and materials, each offering a unique aesthetic. Your creativity can shine as you decide on the arrangement, color palette, and pattern that will define your piece.

Gathering Materials: To start, you'll need the following materials:

- Beads of your choice
- Stringing material (beading wire, silk cord, nylon thread, etc.)
- Clasps or closures
- Beading needles (if using thin stringing materials)
- Beading mat (for organization)

Step-by-Step Bead Stringing Process:

1. **Measure and Cut:** Determine the desired length of your jewelry piece and cut the stringing material accordingly. Be sure to add a few extra inches to account for knots and the clasp.

2. **Attach the Clasp:** Begin by attaching one end of the stringing material to the clasp using a jump ring or a crimp bead. This end will form the beginning of your necklace or bracelet.

3. **Plan and String:** Lay out your beads in the desired order and start threading them onto the stringing material. Pay attention to the pattern, spacing, and balance.

4. **Knotting for Spacing:** Between each bead, you can add knots to create spacing and prevent the beads from rubbing against each other. For added security, place knots on both sides of the bead.

5. **Attaching Components:** If your design includes pendants, charms, or focal beads, incorporate them into the stringing process. Use jump rings to attach them securely.

6. **Closing the Piece:** Once all the beads and components are in place, attach the other end of the stringing material to the clasp. This completes the jewelry piece.

The Knotting Process:

Knotting serves various purposes in bead jewelry making:

- **Spacing Knots:** Prevent beads from rubbing against each other.

- **Functional Knots:** Create adjustable closures for bracelets and necklaces.

- **Decorative Knots:** Add texture and design elements to your piece.

Knot Styles:

- **Overhand Knot:** The simplest knot, great for spacing beads and creating stops.

- **Square Knot:** Used for adjustable closures, offering a balanced appearance.

- **Slip Knot:** Ideal for adjustable closures, making jewelry easy to put on and take off.

- **Lark's Head Knot:** Used to attach components like pendants to cords or chains.

Adjustable Closures: To create adjustable closures, use square knots or slip knots to allow the wearer to customize the length of the piece.

Projects to Demonstrate the Technique:

Elegant Pearl Necklace

Create a timeless and elegant pearl necklace using bead stringing and knotting techniques. This classic piece will add sophistication to any outfit and become a cherished accessory in your collection.

Materials Needed:

- Freshwater pearls (8-10mm)
- Silk thread (matching color)
- Clasp of your choice (lobster clasp, hook-and-eye clasp, etc.)
- Jump rings (if needed)
- Beading mat (optional, for organization)
- Beading needle (optional)

Tools:

- Scissors
- Beading mat (optional)
- Chain-nose pliers (if using jump rings)

Steps:

1. Gather Your Materials: On a clear work surface, arrange your pearls, silk thread, clasp, and any other necessary supplies.

2. Count and Cut: Choose the necklace's preferred length. In order to allow for knotting and the clasp, add a few more inches. To this length, cut the silk thread.

3. Use chain-nose pliers to fasten the clasp to one end of the silk thread if it has a jump ring. You can omit this step if your clasp already has a built-in loop.

4. Pearls: To string the pearls onto the thread, either thread one end of the silk thread through the beading needle (if using), or use your fingers. For a special appearance, make a pattern or combine several sizes.

5. Simply tie an overhand knot after each pearl to create distance and keep the pearls from rubbing against one another.

6. Measure and Space: Thread pearls and tie knots till the necklace is the desired length. To check the fit and make any necessary adjustments, place the strand against your neck.

7. Once you've reached the desired length, fasten the clasp's opposite end. If a jump ring is being used, use chain-nose pliers to secure it to the silk thread.

8. Finishing touches: To guarantee a tight fit, gently draw the knots toward the pearls. Leave a brief tail after cutting any extra silk thread. The cut ends of the silk thread should be covered with a small bit of fray check or clear nail paint to stop it from unraveling.

9. Jump rings can be used to firmly attach the clasp's other end if necessary. Make sure the clasp is appropriately positioned for comfort when wearing.

Boho Leather Bracelet

Create a bohemian-inspired leather bracelet that embodies free-spirited style and showcases your creativity. This bracelet combines leather cord with colorful beads for a unique and eye-catching accessory.

Materials Needed:

- Leather cord (1.5-2mm thickness)
- Assorted beads in different sizes and colors
- Button closure or toggle clasp
- Beading mat (optional, for organization)
- Scissors
- Beading needle (optional)
- Chain-nose pliers (if using jump rings)

Steps:

1. **Gather Your Materials:** Lay out your leather cord, beads, closure, and any tools you'll need on a clean workspace.

2. **Measure and Cut:** Wrap the leather cord around your wrist to determine the desired bracelet length. Add a few extra inches to account for the knots and closure. Cut the leather cord to this length.

3. **Attach the Closure:** If using a button closure, thread one end of the leather cord through the buttonhole and create a loop. If using a toggle clasp, fold one end of the cord over the bar of the clasp and tie a knot to secure it.

4. **Thread the Beads:** Begin threading beads onto the leather cord. Mix and match bead sizes, colors, and textures for a boho look. Create a pattern or go for a random arrangement.

5. **Create Spacing Knots:** After adding a few beads, tie an overhand knot close to the last bead. This will create spacing between the beads and add a rustic touch.

6. **Continue Beading and Knotting:** Alternate between threading beads and tying knots until you're satisfied with the bracelet's design. You can also leave sections of the cord bare for an organic and laid-back feel.

7. **Attach the Other End:** Once you've reached the desired length, attach the other end of the closure. If using a button closure, create a loop and secure it with a knot. If using a toggle clasp, tie a knot to keep the clasp in place.

8. **Adjust the Fit:** Try on the bracelet to ensure it's the desired length. Make any adjustments by loosening or tightening the knots as needed.

9. **Finishing Touches:** Trim any excess leather cord, leaving a short tail. If using a button closure, ensure the loop is securely knotted. Apply a small amount of clear nail polish or fray check to the cut ends to prevent unraveling.

Delicate Birthstone Earrings

Create a pair of delicate birthstone earrings that celebrate personal connections and add a touch of elegance to any outfit. These earrings feature dainty gemstone beads that represent each individual's birth month, making them a thoughtful and meaningful gift.

Materials Needed:

- Beading wire (26 gauge or finer)
- Gemstone beads (birthstone colors)
- Ear wires (French hooks or lever-back)
- Jump rings (if needed)
- Chain-nose pliers
- Round-nose pliers
- Wire cutters

- Beading mat (optional, for organization)

Steps:

1. Gather Your Resources: On a spotless work surface, arrange your gemstone beads, beading wire, ear wires, and any additional materials.

2. Select Birthstone Jewelry: Choose gemstone beads based on your particular preferences or the recipient's birth month. January's birthstone is garnet, February's is amethyst, March's is aquamarine, and so forth.

3. Snip the beading wire: Cut a piece of beading wire to the length you want for your earrings, which is normally 2 to 2.5 inches. For each earring, you'll need two parts that are the same length.

4. Create a design or arrangement that you find visually pleasing by threading gemstone beads onto one end of the beading wire.

5. After threading the beads, create a little loop at the end of the beading wire using round-nose pliers. The beads will be secured by this loop and won't fall off.

6. Wrap the Beads: To hold the beads in place, carefully wrap the beading wire around the loop's base. Several smooth and even wraps should be made around the wire.

7. Trim Extra Wire: Cut any extra beading wire with wire cutters, leaving a brief tail.

8. Use chain-nose pliers to open the loop on the ear wire before attaching it. Place the wrapped bead's loop over the loop of the ear wire and tighten the loop.

9. For the second earring, repeat: To make the second earring, follow the same procedure, making sure that both of them have the same shape and length.

Chunky Statement Necklace

Make a bold fashion statement with a chunky statement necklace that commands attention and showcases your unique style. This eye-catching necklace combines larger beads with a sturdy design, creating a piece that stands out and adds a touch of glamour to any ensemble.

Materials Needed:

- Beading wire (0.018-0.024 inch diameter)

- Large statement beads (assorted sizes and colors)
- Spacer beads (optional)
- Crimp beads (matching color to wire)
- Clasp of your choice (toggle clasp, lobster clasp, etc.)
- Jump rings (if needed)
- Crimping pliers
- Chain-nose pliers
- Wire cutters
- Beading mat (optional, for organization)

Steps:

1. Gather Your Materials: On a neat work surface, arrange your large statement beads, beading wire, clasp, and any other necessary supplies.

2. Selecting Statement Beads To create a vibrant and eye-catching design, choose large beads that are different in size, shape, and color. You can combine gemstone, glass, acrylic, and other types of beads.

3. Cut and measure the beading wire: Choose the necklace's preferred length. To allow for crimps and changes, cut a piece of beading wire that is a few inches longer than the desired necklace length.

4. Link the clasp end: Insert one end of the beading wire through the clasp's opening (toggle or lobster clasp).

Leaving a little loop, thread the wire back through the crimp bead. To secure the clasp, flatten the crimp bead using crimping pliers.

5. Begin by stringing your preferred statement beads onto the beading wire in a pleasing pattern or arrangement. If desired, place spacer beads in between the statement beads.

6. Crimp beads can be used to make space between the statement beads. After every statement bead, attach a crimp bead to the wire and press it against the bead.

7. Secure statement beads and crimp beads by weaving wire through clasp, threading back through final crimp bead, and flattening crimp bead using crimping pliers.

8. Try the necklace on and alter the length by moving the crimp beads up or down as necessary. The necklace should hang properly and at the desired location.

9. Finishing touches: Trim any extra beading wire after you're satisfied with the length. If using a toggle clasp, fasten the closure by using jump rings to join the bar and loop halves of the clasp.

Adjustable Charm Bracelet

Design and create an adjustable charm bracelet that not only showcases your favorite charms but also offers a customizable fit. This versatile bracelet combines charm beads with sliding knots, allowing the wearer to adjust the bracelet's length for comfort and style.

Materials Needed:

- Beading thread (nylon or silk)
- Charm beads of your choice
- Spacer beads (optional)
- Small seed beads or metal beads (for sliding knots)
- Clasp or closure (lobster clasp or jump ring)
- Clear nail polish or fray check
- Scissors
- Ruler
- Beading mat (optional, for organization)

Tools:

- Tapestry needle (large-eye needle)
- Chain-nose pliers (for attaching clasp)

Steps:

1. **Gather Your Materials:** Lay out your charm beads, beading thread, closure, and any other supplies on a clean workspace.

2. **Choose Charm Beads:** Select your favorite charm beads that hold personal meaning or align with your style.

3. **Measure and Cut Thread:** Cut a length of beading thread to approximately 15-20 inches. This length will allow you to create the sliding knots and still have enough thread for beading.

4. **Prepare Sliding Knot Beads:** To create the adjustable aspect of the bracelet, thread a small seed bead or metal bead onto the thread, leaving a 2-3 inch tail.

5. **Thread Charm Beads:** Thread your chosen charm beads onto the thread, creating a pattern or arrangement that appeals to you. Add spacer beads between charm beads if desired.

6. **Slide the Knot Beads:** After adding a few charm beads, slide the thread through another small seed bead or metal bead. This bead will function as a sliding knot and adjust the bracelet's length.

7. **Tie a Sliding Knot:** Form a loop with the thread, passing it through the sliding knot bead again. Gently tighten the loop around the bead to create a sliding knot. This knot should move along the thread easily to adjust the bracelet's length.

8. **Continue Beading and Knotting:** Repeat steps 5-7 until you've threaded all the charm beads and created the desired number of sliding knots for adjustment.

9. **Attach Closure:** Put a clasp or closing on both ends of the thread to complete the bracelet. If a lobster clasp is being used, fasten it directly. If a jump ring is being

used, open it with chain-nose pliers, connect it to the thread loop, and then firmly close the jump ring.

10. **Adjustable Fit:** To wear the bracelet, slide the sliding knots along the thread to adjust the bracelet's length to your liking. Knots should hold their position while allowing for easy adjustment.

Chapter 5: Wire Wrapping.

Wire wrapping is a creative jewelry technique that secures beads, stones, and other components, enhancing the artistic appeal of your designs.

Materials Needed:

- Beads, gemstones, or other components
- Wire (copper, sterling silver, gold-filled, etc.)
- Round-nose pliers
- Chain-nose pliers
- Wire cutters

Steps:

1. Gather the beads, gems, or other elements you'll be wire wrapping before you start. Make sure the beads you choose have holes that can fit the wire gauge you're using.

2. Select Your Wire: For your project, choose the wire gauge (thickness) that is appropriate. While thinner wire enables more detailed designs, thicker wire offers sturdiness.

3. Remove the Wire: Cut a wire piece to the length you want. A typical rule of thumb is to cut 6 to 8 inches of wire, but you should adapt dependent on the size of your project.

4. **Create a Simple Loop:** If your design calls for connecting components, start by using round-nose pliers to make a simple loop at one end of the wire. Beads won't fall off thanks to this loop.

5. **Thread the Beads:** Arrange your beads or other components on the wire by sliding them onto the wire. Place a larger focal bead in the middle of smaller accent beads while making a wrapped pendant.

6. **Place the Beads:** Place the beads on the wire in the desired location. Leave enough room at the wire's end so that you may loop it again.

7. **Start** When wrapping, use chain-nose pliers to hold the wire immediately above the bead. Bend the wire 90 degrees away from the bead using your fingers.

8. Start wrapping the wire by grabbing it immediately above the bend you made with your fingers or a pair of chain-nose pliers. Wrap the wire a total of two to three times around the stem (the wire that is beneath the bead).

9. After forming the wraps, use chain-nose pliers to gently squeeze and tuck any extra wire up against the stem. This will secure the wraps. Make sure the wraps are even and tight.

10. **Create the Second Loop:** Using the leftover wire and round-nose pliers, make a second straightforward loop. The addition of this loop will seal the joint and stop beads from slipping off the other end.

11. Trim Extra Wire: Cut any extra wire with wire cutters, leaving a brief tail. To avoid sharp edges, tuck the trimmed end up against the wrapping.

Five Wire Wrapping Jewelry Projects:

Wire Wrapped Pendant

Materials Needed:

- Focal bead or gemstone
- Wire (20-24 gauge, depending on your design)
- Chain-nose pliers
- Round-nose pliers
- Wire cutters

Steps:

1. **Choose Your Focal Bead:** Select a bead or gemstone that will be the centerpiece of your pendant. Choose a size and shape that appeals to you and complements your design.

2. **Measure and Cut the Wire:** Cut a piece of wire about 6-8 inches long, depending on the size of your pendant and the complexity of your design.

3. **Create a Bail Loop:** Hold the wire about 1-1.5 inches from one end using chain-nose pliers. Bend the wire at a 90-degree angle to create a loop.

4. **Bend the Wire Around the Bead:** Place the looped end of the wire against the top of your focal bead. Wrap the wire around the bead once to secure it in place. This will create the initial connection point.

5. **Create a Twist:** To add a decorative touch, twist the two wire ends together just above the bead. Use chain-nose pliers to grip the wire ends and gently twist them.

6. **Start Wrapping:** Position the twisted section against the top of the bead. Use your fingers or chain-nose pliers to bend the wires at a 90-degree angle away from the bead.

7. **Begin Wrapping the Bail:** With the wires extending upward, start wrapping one of the wires around the other. This will form the bail that your chain or cord will pass through.

8. **Wrap 2-3 Times:** Continue wrapping the wire around the other wire, creating 2-3 tight wraps. Ensure the wraps are neat and even.

9. **Trim the Excess Wire:** Once you've completed the wraps, use wire cutters to trim any excess wire, leaving a small tail.

10. **Tuck the Trimmed End:** Use chain-nose pliers to gently press the trimmed end of the wire against the wraps to prevent any sharp edges.

11. **Shape the Bail:** Use round-nose pliers to gently shape the bail loop to your desired curve. This loop will allow you to attach the pendant to a chain or cord.

12. **Add a Chain or Cord:** Slide a chain or cord through the bail loop to complete your wire-wrapped pendant.

Wire Wrapped Earrings:

This project demonstrates the process of creating wire-wrapped earrings, a unique and intricate jewelry creation featuring beads, gemstones, and wirework, showcasing intricate designs.

Materials Needed:

- Beads or gemstones for dangles
- Ear wires
- Wire (20-24 gauge, depending on your design)
- Chain-nose pliers
- Round-nose pliers
- Wire cutters

Steps:

1. Pick Your Beads: Decide the beads or gemstones you wish to use as the earrings' dangles. Select beads with holes that can fit the wire gauge you plan to use.

2. Cut the Wire: Depending on the size of your beads and your preferred design, cut two lengths of wire that are each about 4-6 inches long.

3. Make a Basic Loop: Chain-nose pliers are used to hold one end of a wire component. To make a loop, bend the wire at a 90-degree angle.

4. Thread the Bead: Thread the wire through the loop you made earlier with one of your chosen beads. Just above the loop, place the bead.

5. Holding the wire and bead together using chain-nose pliers will allow you to bend the wire. Bend the wire 90 degrees away from the bead using your fingers.

6. Form the Dangle: Hold the bent wire tightly against the bead with round-nose pliers. Rotate your wrist while wrapping the wire around the pliers' jaw to create a loop.

7. Complete the Loop: Keep rotating your wrist until the wire has completely encircled itself. Make sure the loop is symmetrical and centered.

8. Trim Extra Wire: Cut any extra wire with wire cutters, leaving a brief tail. To avoid sharp edges, tuck the trimmed end up against the wrapping.

9. Repeat for the Second Dangle: Using the second piece of wire and a different bead, repeat steps 3 through 8 to make a second dangle.

10. Open the Ear Wire: Carefully pry open the loop of an ear wire using chain-nose pliers. To keep the shape of the loop, open it sideways.

11. Dangles are attached by sliding their loops onto the free loop of the ear wire. Make sure the dangles are straight and hang freely.

12. Seal the Ear Wire: Using chain-nose pliers, carefully and firmly close the ear wire's loop.

Wire Wrapped Ring

This project teaches you how to create a wire-wrapped gemstone ring, showcasing its unique design and allowing you to craft a personalized piece of jewelry.

Materials Needed:

- Gemstone or bead for the ring focal point
- Wire (20-24 gauge, depending on your design)
- Ring mandrel or cylindrical object
- Chain-nose pliers
- Round-nose pliers
- Wire cutters

Steps:

1. Choose a gemstone or bead to serve as the center of attention for your ring. Pick a shape and size that work with your design.

2. Remove the Wire: Depending on the complexity of your design and the size of the gemstone, cut a piece of wire 6 to 8 inches long.

3. Creating the Ring Base Place the wire around the ring mandrel at the chosen ring size if using one. If utilizing a cylindrical object, make a ring shape by wrapping the wire around it.

4. Twist the wire: At the back of the ring, twist the wire's two ends together. This will produce the ring's band.

5. Make a Basic Loop: Using chain-nose pliers, grasp one of the ends of the twisted wire. To make a loop, bend the wire at a 90-degree angle.

6. Slide the gemstone through the loop you made in the wire to thread it. Put the gem at the loop's topmost position.

7. With chain-nose pliers, hold the wire and gemstone together while bending it. Bend the wire 90 degrees away from the gemstone using your fingers.

8. Create the Loop: Hold the bent wire tightly against the gem with a pair of round-nosed pliers. Rotate your wrist while wrapping the wire around the pliers' jaw to create a loop.

9. Round the loop: Once the wire has completely encircled and looped over itself, keep turning your wrist. Make sure the loop is symmetrical and centered.

10. Trim Extra Wire: Cut any extra wire with wire cutters, leaving a brief tail. To avoid sharp edges, tuck the trimmed end up against the wrapping.

11. Adjust the Ring Size: Place the gemstone in the preferred location by sliding it down onto the ring band. By gently contracting or expanding the twisted wire ends, you can change the ring size.

12. Secure the Gemstone: Raise the gemstone back up and, holding it in place with chain-nose pliers, gently push the twisted wire ends on the gem's back.

Wire Wrapped Bracelet:

This project demonstrates the use of wire wrapping in crafting unique jewelry pieces, including a wire-wrapped bracelet, by combining wirework with beads.

Materials Needed:

- Beads for the bracelet
- Wire (20-24 gauge, depending on your design)
- Clasp and jump rings (optional)
- Chain-nose pliers
- Round-nose pliers
- Wire cutters

Steps:

1. Select the beads you want to use for your bracelet from your selection. Select beads with holes that can fit the wire gauge you plan to use.

2. Cut the Wire: Depending on the length of your bracelet and the number of beads, cut a piece of wire that is 8 to 10 inches long.

3. Make a Basic Loop: Chain-nose pliers are used to hold one end of the wire. To make a loop, bend the wire at a 90-degree angle.

4. Thread the Beads: Slide the beads through the loop you made on the wire. Put the beads on the bracelet in the desired positions.

5. Use chain-nose pliers to hold the wire and beads together while bending the wire. Bend the wire 90 degrees away from the beads using your fingers.

6. Make a Bead Link by grabbing the bent wire closely to the beads using round-nose pliers. Rotate your wrist while wrapping the wire around the pliers' jaw to create a loop.

7. Complete the Loop: Keep rotating your wrist until the wire has completely encircled itself. Make sure the loop is symmetrical and centered.

8. Trim Extra Wire: Cut any extra wire with wire cutters, leaving a brief tail. To avoid sharp edges, tuck the trimmed end up against the wrapping.

9. Repetition for Every Bead For each bead in the bracelet, repeat steps 3 through 8 to form individual bead links.

10. Link the Beads Together: By slightly opening the loops with chain-nose pliers and sliding one loop into the other, you may join the bead links together. Securely close the loops.

11. Add a Clasp (Optional): Use jump rings to connect a clasp to the bracelet's ends. Chain-nose pliers are used to open the jump rings, which are then closed after the clasp is fastened.

Wire Wrapped Necklace:

Creating a wire-wrapped necklace is a fantastic way to express your creativity and design a unique piece of jewelry. Wire wrapping allows you to combine beads, gemstones, and wirework to craft a necklace that reflects your personal style. In this project, we'll guide you through the steps to make a wire-wrapped bead necklace with a focal pendant.

Materials Needed:

- Beads for the necklace
- Focal pendant or bead
- Wire (20-24 gauge, depending on your design)
- Chain or cord

- Clasp and jump rings (optional)
- Chain-nose pliers
- Round-nose pliers
- Wire cutters

Steps:

1. Select the beads you want to use for your necklace from your selection. To add visual appeal, use a range of shapes, sizes, and colors.

2. Choose a Focal Pendant: Decide on a focal pendant or a sizable bead that will act as the necklace's focal point. Wire-wrapped, this pendant will hang from the chain or cable.

3. Cut the Wire: Depending on the size of the pendant and the quantity of beads, cut a piece of wire that is between 10 and 12 inches long.

4. Make a Basic Loop: Chain-nose pliers are used to hold one end of the wire. To make a loop, bend the wire at a 90-degree angle.

5. Thread the Beads: Slide the beads through the loop you made on the wire. To make a design that looks appealing, mix and match the colors, sizes, and shapes of the beads.

6. Use chain-nose pliers to hold the wire and beads together while bending the wire. Bend the wire 90 degrees away from the beads using your fingers.

7. Make a Bead Link by grabbing the bent wire closely to the beads using round-nose pliers. Rotate your wrist while wrapping the wire around the pliers' jaw to create a loop.

8. Round the loop: Once the wire has completely encircled and looped over itself, keep turning your wrist. Make sure the loop is symmetrical and centered.

9. Trim Extra Wire: Cut any extra wire with wire cutters, leaving a brief tail. To avoid sharp edges, tuck the trimmed end up against the wrapping.

10. Repetition for Every Bead For each bead in the necklace, repeat steps 3 through 9 to form individual bead links.

11. Wire-wrap the Pendant: To attach the focal pendant to the necklace, use the same wire-wrapping technique. The pendant should have a loop at the top so that it may be fastened to the necklace.

12. The bead links are joined together by using chain-nose pliers to slightly expand the loops and sliding one loop into the other. Securely close the loops.

13. Add a Clasp (Optional): Use jump rings to connect a clasp to the ends of the necklace. Chain-nose pliers are used to open the jump rings, which are then closed after the clasp is fastened.

14. Add Chain or Cord: To finish your design, add a chain or cord to the ends of the necklace.

Chapter 6: Craft Your Jewels.

Here are several projects for various jewels that beginners can craft.

1. Earrings

Cuffed Earrings with Beads

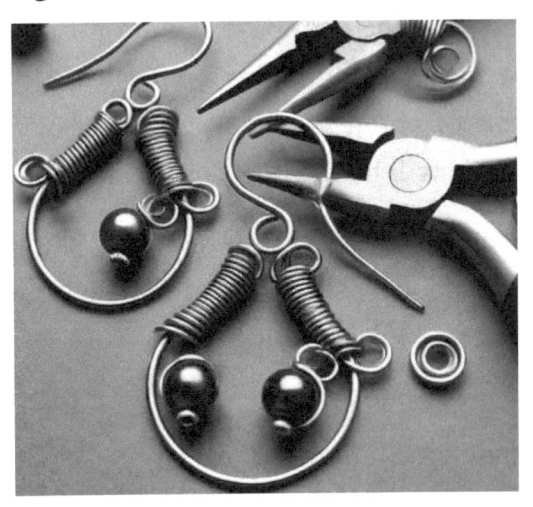

Materials Needed:

- Wire (20-24 gauge, preferably in a color that complements your beads)
- Beads of your choice (small to medium-sized)
- Chain-nose pliers
- Round-nose pliers
- Wire cutters

Steps:

1. Get Your Materials Ready: assemble your pliers, wire, and beads. Select beads that go with your sense of fashion as well as the color of your wire.

2. Measure the wire and cut it: Depending on the intended size of the cuff and the quantity of beads you intend to use, cut a piece of wire measuring around 6 to 8 inches.

3. How to Make the Cuff Base: Chain-nose pliers are used to hold one end of the wire. To create a little loop with a diameter of about 1/4 inch, bend the wire at a slight angle. This will be the beginning place for the cuff.

4. First Bead to be Added: Place a bead slightly above the loop you made by sliding it onto the wire. The bead will be positioned in the middle of the cuff.

5. Creating the First Loop Chain-nose pliers are used to hold the wire and bead together. Bend the wire 90 degrees away from the bead using your fingers.

6. Making the Loop Close to the bead, grasp the bent wire with a pair of round-nosed pliers. Rotate your wrist while wrapping the wire around the pliers' jaw to create a loop.

7. Complete the Loop: Keep rotating your wrist until the wire has completely encircled itself. The size of this loop should be greater than the initial loop.

8. Additional Beads: Alongside the first bead, slide more beads onto the wire. For a variable appearance, you might make a pattern or utilize various bead sizes.

9. Repeat Looping: Repeat steps 5 through 7 to make loops on both sides of each additional bead. These loops will serve to anchor the beads and create the cuff's framework.

10. Continue Beading and Looping: Continue adding beads and making loops until the length of the cuff that you want is achieved. By making loops on both sides of every bead, you can ensure that symmetry is maintained.

11. Create a final loop at the other end of the cuff to secure the last bead once you have added all of your beads and loops.

12. Trim Extra Wire: Cut any extra wire with wire cutters, leaving a brief tail. To avoid sharp edges, tuck the trimmed end up against the wrapping.

13. Pattern Variation: Feel free to play around with the bead and loop arrangement to achieve the look you're going for.

14. Create a matching pair of cuff earrings for the other ear by repeating the method.

Beaded Earrings

Materials Needed:

- Beads of your choice (small to medium-sized)
- Ear wires
- Beading wire or thread
- Beading needle (if using thread)
- Crimp beads (if using wire)
- Crimping pliers (if using wire)
- Chain-nose pliers
- Round-nose pliers
- Wire cutters

Steps:

1. Choose Your Beads: Opt for beads that go with your personal style and preferred earring style. To add more

visual interest, you can choose uniform beads or mix beads of various sizes and colors.

2. Create a Design Plan: To see how your earrings will look, arrange your beads. Choose the pattern and layout you want to use.

3. If using beading wire, string the beads by slipping them onto the wire in the planned sequence. If using thread, string the beads onto the thread with a beading needle.

4. Bead Pattern Creation: Make sure the length of the beads matches the size of the earrings you want, then string them in the required pattern according to your design.

5. Finishing the Ends: If you're using beading wire, fit a crimp bead and an ear wire loop onto the end of the wire. Leaving a tiny loop of wire between the crimp bead and the ear wire, loop the wire back through the crimp bead. To secure the crimp bead and cut any extra wire, use crimping pliers.

6. Make Bead Dangles (Optional): Slide a bead onto a headpin, leaving space for a loop, if you want to add dangling beads. Make a loop at the top of the headpin using round-nose pliers, then fasten the loop to the ear wire before closing the headpin.

7. Repeat for the Second Earring: To make the second earring, repeat steps 3 through 6 while making sure that both earrings have the same style and length.

8. Examine and correct: Make sure the earrings are symmetrical and the beads are fastened. Adjust as necessary to make sure they hang evenly.

Bottle Cap Earrings

Materials Needed:

- Bottle caps (cleaned and sanitized)
- Decorative paper, fabric, or images
- Clear epoxy resin or dimensional glaze
- Earring hooks
- Jump rings (optional)
- Chain-nose pliers
- Round-nose pliers
- Scissors or craft knife
- Adhesive (such as glue or double-sided tape)

Steps:

1. Start with clean and sterilized bottle caps while preparing the caps. To make sure they are safe to wear, remove any residue or sharp edges.

2. Cut Ornamental Paper: To suit the inside diameter of the bottle caps, cut decorative paper, cloth, or graphics. The backgrounds for your earrings will be these.

3. The cut paper or image should be adhered to the interior of the bottle cap using adhesive (glue or double-sided tape). Ensure that it is flat and centered.

4. Combine the Resin: If using epoxy resin, mix the resin and hardener according to the manufacturer's instructions. This step is optional if using dimensional glaze.

5. Applying a glaze or resin Pour a tiny bit of resin into each bottle cap, filling the cap and covering the background. Squeeze a coat of dimensional glaze onto the backdrop if using it.

6. Remove Air Bubbles: To get rid of air bubbles, gently tap the bottle caps against a surface. Any bubbles that rise to the surface can then be popped with a toothpick.

7. Follow the resin manufacturer's directions for the recommended curing period. If you're using dimensional glaze, make sure to follow the product's drying instructions.

8. Use chain-nose pliers to open the loop on the earring hook before attaching it. Utilizing the pliers, fasten the loop to the opening in the bottle cap.

9. Repeat for the Second Earring: To make the second earring, repeat steps 1 through 8 while making sure that both earrings have the same style and size.

10. Add Jump Rings (Optional): Before connecting the earring hook to the bottle cap, you can, if you'd like, add a jump ring to it. This can give the earrings movement and additional flair.

11. Check and Adjust: Make sure the optional jump rings and the earring hooks are securely fastened to the bottle cap earrings. Make **any symmetry and comfort modifications required.**

Tassel Earrings

Materials needed:

- Embroidery thread or silk thread
- Earring hooks
- Jump rings.
- Pliers
- Scissors

Instructions:

- Fold the embroidery thread you are using in half.
- Use a jump ring to connect the thread's folded end to an earring hook.
- Starting with your fingers, tightly wrap the thread around them, leaving a tiny loop at the top.
- Carefully slide the looped end off your fingers once you've reached the proper thickness.
- To shape the tassel, cut through the bottom loops and trim any crooked ends.
- The tassel can be fastened to an earring hook by first adding a jump ring to the top of it.
- To make the second earring, repeat the procedure.

Geometric Clay Earrings

Materials needed:

- various colored polymer clay

- jewelry hooks
- a rolling pin
- Craft knife
- baking pan
- Textured paper
- Super glue

Instructions:

- Using a rolling pin, flatten the polymer clay into a thin sheet.
- Cut out geometrical forms like triangles, squares, or circles using a craft knife.
- Create a hole for the earring hook at the top of each shape.
- On a baking sheet covered with parchment paper, put the clay shapes.
- In accordance with the directions on the packaging, bake the clay.
- Use super glue to affix the earring hooks after the clay has cooled.
- Before putting on the earrings, let the glue entirely cure.

Beaded Hoop Earrings

Materials needed:

- Hoops of metal earrings
- choose your own beads.
- necklace wire
- Flat-nosed pliers
- Cutters for wire

Instructions:

- Choose your desired beads, then string them onto a piece of jewelry wire.
- Starting at one end, wrap the wire around the earring hoop.
- As you add beads, keep carefully wrapping the wire around the hoop.
- Trim any extra wire when you get to the other end of the hoop, and then use the pliers to secure the end.

- Steps for the second earring should be repeated.

Feather Earrings

Materials needed:

- Feathers
- jewelry hooks
- Pliers, scissors, and jump rings.

Instructions:

- Trim two feathers to the appropriate length using feathers of equal size.
- Using pliers, fasten a jump ring to the peak of each feather.
- Open a different jump ring, then thread it through the jump rings on the earring hook and the feather.
- Using the pliers, tightly close the jump ring.
- To make the second earring, repeat the procedure.

Leather Fringe Earrings

Materials needed:

- Leather or faux leather
- Earring hooks
- Jump rings
- Pliers
- Scissors
- Hole punch

Instructions:

- Cut the leather into fringe-like pieces or thin strips.
- Make a hole at the top of each strip or piece of fringe using a hole punch.
- Using pliers, insert a jump ring through the opening and join it to the earring hook.
- To make the second earring, repeat the procedure.

2. Rings

Button Ring

Materials:

- Button (with a shank or a flat back)
- Ring base or adjustable ring finding
- Jewelry adhesive or glue

Instructions:

- Apply a small amount of jewelry adhesive or glue to the back of the button.
- Press the button onto the ring base or adjustable ring finding.
- Allow the adhesive to dry according to the product instructions before wearing the ring.

Ribbon Wrapped Ring

Materials

- Ring base or adjustable ring finding
- Ribbon or fabric strip
- Scissors
- Jewelry adhesive or glue

Instructions:

1. Apply a small amount of jewelry adhesive or glue to the ring base or adjustable ring finding.

2. Place the end of the ribbon or fabric strip onto the adhesive and start wrapping it around the ring base.

3. Continue wrapping the ribbon or fabric tightly around the base, making sure to cover the entire surface.

4. When you reach the end, apply a little more adhesive or glue to secure the ribbon in place.

5. If necessary, cut off any extra fabric or ribbon.

6. Allow the adhesive to dry according to the product instructions before wearing the ring.

Sterling Silver Ring

Materials Needed:

- Sterling silver sheet or wire (18-20 gauge)
- Jeweler's saw or metal snips
- Jewelry file set
- Steel ring mandrel
- Rawhide or nylon mallet
- Sandpaper or emery paper (various grits)
- Liver of sulfur or blackening solution (optional)
- Polishing cloth or jewelry polishing tools

Steps:

1. **Design Your Ring:** Decide on the style and width of your ring. You can create a plain band or add texture, patterns, or even a bezel-set stone.

2. **Measure and Cut the Silver:** Measure your finger or the intended wearer's finger to determine the ring size. Cut

a piece of sterling silver sheet or wire that's slightly longer than the circumference of the finger and wide enough for the desired ring width.

3. **Shape the Silver:** Using metal snips or a jeweler's saw, cut the silver to the desired length. If creating a textured band, use files to shape and refine the edges.

4. **Form the Ring Band:** Place the cut silver piece on a steel ring mandrel. Use a rawhide or nylon mallet to gently shape the silver around the mandrel to form the basic ring band shape. Ensure it's the correct size and shape for the finger.

5. **Solder the Seam (Optional):** If working with a silver sheet, you can solder the seam to create a continuous band. This requires soldering skills and equipment.

6. **Refine the Shape:** Take the shaped band off the mandrel and use files to refine the shape, ensuring it's smooth and even. Use progressively finer grits of sandpaper or emery paper to further smooth the edges and surface.

7. **Add Texture or Pattern (Optional):** If desired, use various tools to add texture, patterns, or designs to the surface of the ring.

8. **Blacken and Polish (Optional):** If you want an oxidized or aged look, use liver of sulfur or a blackening solution to darken the metal. Polish the raised areas to reveal the contrast. Alternatively, you can skip this step for a polished silver look.

9. **Final Polishing:** Use polishing cloths or jewelry polishing tools to achieve a high shine on the silver. Pay attention to the inside and outside of the ring.

10. **Check Size and Comfort:** Slide the finished ring onto the intended finger to check for size and comfort. Make any necessary adjustments.

Wire Wrapped Crystal Ring:

Materials Needed:

- Crystal bead or gemstone cabochon
- Jewelry wire (20-24 gauge)
- Ring mandrel or cylindrical object
- Wire cutters
- Round-nose pliers
- Chain-nose pliers

Steps:

1. Choose a Crystal Bead: For the focal point of your ring, pick a crystal bead or cabochon of a precious stone.

2. Cut Wire: Depending on the size of your gem and ring size, cut a length of jewelry wire that is 6 to 8 inches long.

3. Grasp one end of the wire with a pair of round-nose pliers, then roll the wire around the pliers to form a loop.

4. encircle the wire: Place the crystal bead in the center of the loop after sliding it onto the wire. To secure the crystal in place, begin looping the wire around the crystal and loop.

5. To create the ring shank, place the crystal and wrapped loop on the ring mandrel or any cylindrical piece that fits the size of the ring you want to make. To build the ring's shank, carefully wrap the wire around the mandrel.

6. Once you're satisfied with the ring size, adjust and secure it by wrapping the wire around the shank a couple more times to add a decorative pattern. To tightly tuck the wire end, use chain-nose pliers.

7. Final touches: Trim any extra wire with wire cutters. To make the wire wraps snug and secure, adjust them.

Stamped Personalized Name Ring:

Materials Needed:

- Metal blank ring base
- Metal stamping letters or alphabet stamps
- Stamping block or anvil
- Hammer
- Stamp enamel or marker (optional)
- Jewelry file or sandpaper (optional)

Steps:

1. **Choose Ring Base:** Select a metal blank ring base in the desired size and metal (e.g., sterling silver, copper, brass).

2. **Plan Name:** Decide on the name or word you want to stamp onto the ring.

3. **Stamp Letters:** Arrange the metal stamping letters on the ring base to spell out the name or word. Place the ring on a stamping block or anvil.

4. **Stamping Process:** Firmly strike each letter with a hammer to create impressions on the metal. Apply even pressure to ensure clear and consistent stamping.

5. **Color the Letters (Optional):** Use stamp enamel or a permanent marker to darken the stamped letters, enhancing visibility.

6. **Refine Edges (Optional):** Use a jewelry file or sandpaper to smooth and refine the edges of the ring base if desired.

Wrapped Bead Adjustable Ring:

Materials Needed:

- Bead of your choice
- Jewelry wire (20-24 gauge)
- Adjustable ring base
- Wire cutters
- Round-nose pliers
- Chain-nose pliers

Steps:

1. Choose a Bead: Decide which bead will serve as the focal point of your ring.

2. Cut Wire: Depending on the size of your bead and ring base, cut a piece of jewelry wire that is between 4 and 6 inches long.

3. Grasp one end of the wire with a pair of round-nose pliers, then roll the wire around the pliers to form a loop.

4. Bead Threading: Position the chosen bead in the center of the loop by sliding it onto the wire.

5. Wrap the Wire: To hold the bead in place, bring both wire ends together above the bead and wrap them around the bead several times.

6. Attach to Adjustable Ring Base: Thread the wire through the loop or hole in the adjustable ring base to fasten the wrapped bead to the ring.

7. Change the ring size: To alter the ring's size and guarantee a tight fit, gently bend the wire ends.

8. Secure the Wire: Twist the wire ends collectively with chain-nose pliers, making sure they are firmly connected to the ring base.

3. Necklaces

Diamond Drop Necklace

Materials Needed:

- Diamond pendant or gemstone of your choice
- Chain (sterling silver, gold, or the metal of your preference)
- Jump rings
- Clasp (lobster clasp, spring ring clasp, or toggle clasp)
- Chain-nose pliers
- Round-nose pliers
- Wire cutters

Steps:

1. Choose a Diamond Pendant: Opt for a diamond pendant that matches your preferences and style. A solitary diamond, a gemstone put in a setting, or a delicate pattern that catches your eye can all be used as the pendant.

2. Choose a chain that goes well with the pendant and the desired style. Choose a chain style (thin, box, cable) and metal color (silver, gold, or rose gold) that best complements the pendant.

3. Measure the chain and cut it: Add a few additional inches to the desired necklace length to allow for alterations and the clasp. To cut the chain to the required length, use wire cutters.

4. Open a jump ring with chain-nose pliers to attach the clasp. Place the clasp and one end of the chain on the jump ring, then firmly fasten the jump ring.

5. Open a second jump ring, then insert the chain's opposite end and, if necessary, the bail of the pendant onto it to attach the pendant. To secure the pendant to the chain, tightly close the jump ring.

6. Measure the length by holding the necklace around your neck. Open the jump ring that connects the clasp and chain, eliminating any extra chain links, and make any necessary changes.

7. When you are satisfied with the length of the necklace, tightly close the jump ring that connects the clasp to the chain.

8. The time has come to wear and enjoy your diamond drop necklace. It is appropriate for many different events because of its ageless beauty and understated elegance.

Photo Pendants Necklace

Materials Needed:

- Small photo prints or images
- Clear glass cabochons or photo pendants (available at craft stores)
- Jewelry bails (small metal loops that attach to the back of pendants)
- Chain (sterling silver, gold, or the metal of your preference)
- Jump rings
- Clasp (lobster clasp, spring ring clasp, or toggle clasp)
- E6000 adhesive or clear craft glue
- Chain-nose pliers
- Round-nose pliers
- Wire cutters

Steps:

1. Choose Your Photos: Decide the pictures you wish to use as pendants. These can be images of dear ones,

memorable occasions, or anything else with sentimental worth.

2. Selecting Pendants: Choose photo pendants or clear glass cabochons that are the right size for your pictures. Typically, these pendants have a flat side and a rounded side.

3. Photos should be resized and cropped to fit the pendants' specifications. Print the pictures yourself or have them professionally printed. Trim the images to fit the pendants' dimensions and shape.

4. Attach Bails: To secure little jewelry bails to the back of the photo pendants, use E6000 adhesive or transparent craft glue. The pendants can be connected to the chain using the bails.

5. Open Jump Rings: Use chain-nose pliers to unlock a jump ring. One of the photo pendants' bail should be connected to the jump ring.

6. Slide the open jump ring onto the chain to attach the pendant, then use the pliers to firmly close the jump ring. The chain is now fastened to the pendant.

7. Repeat for Additional Pendants: For every additional pendant you want to add to the necklace, repeat steps 5 and 6.

8. Open a jump ring, place the clasp on one end of the chain, and close the jump ring. Securely close the jump ring.

9. Hold the necklace around your neck to check the length and make any necessary adjustments. Open the jump ring that connects the clasp and chain, eliminating any extra chain links, and make any necessary changes.

10. Put On and Enjoy: Your necklace with photo pendants is now ready to be worn and treasured. It's a wonderful way to stay connected to your loved ones.

A Matching Earring And Necklace

Materials Needed:

- Earring components (ear wires, beads, charms, etc.)
- Necklace components (chain, pendant, beads, etc.)
- Jump rings
- Chain-nose pliers
- Round-nose pliers
- Wire cutters

Steps:

1. **Choose Your Design:** Decide on the overall style and theme of your earring and necklace set. Consider factors such as color scheme, bead types, and overall aesthetics.

2. **Select Components:** Choose earring components such as ear wires, beads, charms, or pendants that align with your design. Similarly, select necklace components

including a chain, pendant, beads, and any additional elements.

3. **Plan the Design:** Lay out your chosen components to visualize the design of both the earrings and the necklace. Make sure the components match in terms of style and color.

4. **Create Earrings:** Assemble the earring components according to your design. Use chain-nose and round-nose pliers to open and close jump rings for attaching beads, charms, or pendants. Attach the completed components to ear wires.

5. **Craft the Necklace:** Assemble the necklace components based on your design. Attach the pendant to the chain using jump rings, and add any beads or accents as desired.

6. **Check for Consistency:** Ensure that the design elements and colors of both the earrings and the necklace are consistent and complementary to create a harmonious set.

7. **Wear and Enjoy:** Your matching earring and necklace set is now ready to be worn and admired. Whether for a special occasion or everyday wear, this coordinated set adds a touch of sophistication to your style.

Simple Beaded Necklace

Materials Needed:

- Beads of your choice
- Beading thread or beading wire
- Clasp (lobster clasp, spring ring clasp, or toggle clasp)
- Jump rings
- Crimp beads (if using beading wire)
- Beading needle (if using beading thread)
- Beading pliers (optional)
- Scissors

Steps:

1. Choose Beads: Decide the beads you want to use in your necklace. You can use only one kind of bead or combine beads of various sizes and hues.

2. Count and Cut: Cut a piece of beading thread or beading wire slightly longer than the required length of the necklace.

3. If using beading wire, attach the clasp by first sliding a crimp bead and then one end of the clasp onto the wire. Making a tiny loop around the clasp, loop the wire back through the crimp bead. To secure the clasp, flatten the crimp bead using crimping pliers. Remove any extra wire. Use a jump ring to secure the clasp if you're using thread.

4. Strands of beads: Your chosen beads should be threaded onto the wire or beading thread. You can arrange things in a random or repetitive pattern.

5. After you've finished adding all the beads, affix the clasp's opposite end with a jump ring or a crimp bead (for beading wire) (for thread).

6. Measure the length of the necklace around your neck to make sure it is the right length. By opening the jump ring or crimp bead and adding or removing beads, make any necessary modifications.

7. If you're using beading thread, secure the end by weaving it back through multiple beads to form a tight loop. Remove any extra thread. If you're using beading wire, crimp the end first, then add the jump ring or clasp. Utilizing crimping pliers, flatten the crimp bead and cut any extra wire.

8. Use beading pliers as a finishing touch to make sure jump rings are tightly closed and crimp beads are flattened.

9. Put On and Enjoy: You can now wear and enjoy your plain beaded necklace. It is an adaptable accessory that goes well with many different outfits.

Customized Name Necklace

Materials Needed:

- Metal letter beads (or alphabet charms)
- Spacer beads (optional)
- Chain of your choice
- Jump rings
- Clasp (lobster clasp, spring ring clasp, or toggle clasp)
- Chain-nose pliers
- Round-nose pliers
- Wire cutters

Steps:

1. **Choose Your Name or Word:** Decide on the name, word, or message you want to feature on your necklace. Keep in mind the length of the chain and the size of the beads.

2. **Select Letter Beads:** Choose metal letter beads that spell out your chosen name or word. You can also use alphabet charms if you prefer.

3. **Prepare Spacer Beads (Optional):** If desired, select spacer beads that complement the letter beads. Spacer beads can add a stylish touch and help separate the letters.

4. **Measure Chain Length:** Measure the desired length for your necklace and cut a piece of chain accordingly. Keep in mind that the length includes both the name/word and any additional space you want.

5. **Attach Clasp:** Use chain-nose pliers to attach one end of the chain to the clasp using a jump ring.

6. **Arrange Letter Beads:** Lay out the letter beads on a flat surface in the order of your chosen name/word. If using spacer beads, place them between the letter beads.

7. **Attach Letter Beads:** Use jump rings to attach each letter bead to the chain. Open a jump ring, slide the jump ring through the hole in the letter bead, and attach it to the chain. Close the jump ring securely using pliers.

8. **Check Spacing:** As you attach the letter beads, make sure they are evenly spaced and centered on the chain.

9. **Attach Other End of Chain:** Once all the letter beads are attached, use chain-nose pliers to attach the other end of the chain to the clasp using a jump ring.

10. **Final Touches:** Use pliers to ensure all jump rings are securely closed. Check the necklace's length and adjust if needed.

11. **Wear and Showcase:** Your customized name necklace is now ready to be worn and proudly displayed. It's a piece of jewelry that holds personal significance and reflects your individuality.

4. Bracelets

Beaded Stretch Bracelet:

Materials Needed:

- Stretch cord or elastic cord
- Beads of your choice
- Scissors

Steps:

1. **Select Beads:** Choose the beads you'd like to use for your bracelet. You can use a single type of bead or mix different sizes and colors.

2. **Measure Cord:** Cut a piece of stretch cord about 2-3 inches longer than your desired bracelet size.

3. **String Beads:** Begin stringing the beads onto the cord in your preferred pattern. You can create a repeating pattern or random arrangement.

4. **Create a Knot:** After adding the beads, hold the cord ends together and tie a double knot to secure the beads in place.

5. **Stretch and Knot:** Gently stretch the bracelet to ensure it's comfortable to wear. Tie another double knot to secure the bracelet and trim any excess cord.

6. **Finishing Touch:** Apply a drop of clear nail polish or jewelry glue to the knots to provide extra security. Allow it to dry before wearing.

Leather Wrap Bracelet:

Materials Needed:

- Leather cord or suede cord
- Beads or charms

- Button or clasp
- Scissors
- Jewelry adhesive (optional)

Steps:

1. **Measure Cord:** Cut a length of leather cord about 3 times the desired bracelet length.

2. **Attach Button:** About 1 inch from one end of the cord, fold it in half and attach a button using a square knot. This will be the closure for your bracelet.

3. **String Beads:** String beads or charms onto the cord as desired, leaving space between each bead.

4. **Wrap and String:** Begin wrapping the cord around your wrist, passing the beads through the looped end. Continue wrapping until the desired length is achieved.

5. **Secure Button:** Once you've reached the desired length, pass the button through the loop on the opposite end to secure the bracelet.

6. **Trim Excess Cord:** Trim any excess cord from both ends of the bracelet, leaving a short tail to prevent unraveling.

7. **Finishing Touch:** Optionally, apply a small amount of jewelry adhesive to the knots for added security.

Chain and Charm Bracelet:

Materials Needed:

- Chain of your choice
- Charms or pendants
- Jump rings
- Clasp
- Chain-nose pliers
- Round-nose pliers
- Wire cutters

Steps:

1. Chain Measurement: Make sure the chain is a comfortable fit by measuring it to the size of your wrist.

2. Clasp Attachment: Using chain-nose pliers, attach a clasp to one end of the chain using jump rings.

3. Add Charms: Use jump rings to connect the chain to the charms or pendants of your choice. They are uniformly spaced along the chain.

4. Check the length and make any adjustments to allow room for the charms.

5. Clasp Attachment: Join the chain's opposite end to the other half of the clasp.

6. Use pliers as a finishing touch to make sure all jump rings are shut tightly. You can now put on your charm bracelet.

Macramé Friendship Bracelet:

Materials Needed:

- Colored embroidery floss or cord
- Scissors

Steps:

1. **Cut Strands:** Cut several strands of embroidery floss, each about 2-3 times the desired bracelet length. Fold them in half and create a loop at the top.

2. **Begin Knotting:** Divide the strands into two groups. Start knotting using a half square knot by crossing the left group over the right and looping it under the right group, then pulling the right group through the loop.

3. **Continue Knotting:** Alternate the knotting direction, creating a row of knots. This forms the base for your bracelet.

4. **Add Beads (Optional):** If desired, string beads onto one or more strands before knotting them.

5. **Create Pattern:** Experiment with different knotting patterns, such as chevrons, stripes, or diagonal designs.

6. **Finish with a Knot:** Once your bracelet is the desired length, finish with a final knot and trim any excess strands.

Wire-Wrapped Bangle Bracelet:

Materials Needed:

- Bangle base (metal or acrylic)
- Craft wire (20-24 gauge)
- Beads or charms
- Round-nose pliers
- Chain-nose pliers
- Wire cutters

Steps:

1. **Choose Beads:** Select beads or charms to embellish your bangle bracelet.

2. **Start Wrapping:** Hold the craft wire against the bangle near the opening. Begin wrapping the wire around the bangle to secure it.

3. **Add Beads:** Thread beads onto the wire as you continue wrapping. Position them where you want them on the bangle.

4. **Wrap and Secure:** Continue wrapping the wire around the bangle, passing over the beads to hold them in place.

5. **Create a Design:** Experiment with different bead placement and wire patterns to create your desired design.

6. **Finish Wrapping:** When you've reached the desired design, cut the wire and use chain-nose pliers to tuck the end securely under the wrapped wire.

7. **Repeat for Charms (Optional):** If using charms, attach them to the bangle using jump rings.

8. **Final Touches:** Use pliers to ensure any cut wire ends are tucked in and not poking out.

Now that you've made these original decorations, there are many thoughtful and imaginative ways to use and appreciate them:

1. **Wear Them:** The most obvious way to enjoy your crafted jewelry is to wear it proudly. Whether it's a necklace, bracelet, ring, or earrings, wearing your creations adds a personal touch to your style.

2. **Gifts for Loved Ones:** Handcrafted jewelry makes for heartfelt gifts. Consider gifting your creations to friends, family members, or special someone. Customized pieces, birthstone jewelry, or pieces with sentimental significance can be particularly meaningful.

3. **Special Occasions:** Your crafted jewelry can be the perfect accessory for special occasions like weddings, birthdays, anniversaries, and parties. Match your creations to your outfit or create pieces that align with the theme of the event.

4. **Create a Collection:** If you enjoy jewelry making, why not create a collection over time? You can design pieces that follow a common theme, color palette, or style. This can be a fun way to express your creativity and showcase your evolving skills.

5. **Sell Your Jewelry:** If you've developed a knack for jewelry making, you might consider selling your creations. Online platforms, local craft fairs, and artisan

markets are great places to showcase and sell your handcrafted jewelry.

6. **Swap or Trade:** Connect with fellow jewelry enthusiasts and artists to swap or trade pieces. This can be a wonderful way to diversify your collection and make connections in the creative community.

7. **Host Workshops:** Share your knowledge and passion by hosting jewelry-making workshops for friends, family, or community groups. Teaching others your skills can be incredibly rewarding and provide opportunities for social interaction.

8. **Personalize Gifts:** Incorporate your crafted jewelry into other gifts. For instance, add a handmade bracelet to a wrapped package or attach a pair of earrings to a bouquet of flowers.

9. **Create Memories:** Your jewelry can serve as a lasting memory of a significant event, achievement, or journey. You might create a piece to commemorate a travel adventure or a milestone in your life.

10. **Accessorize Your Home:** Jewelry isn't limited to personal wear. Use your jewelry creations as decorative elements in your home. Hang necklaces on hooks or create a jewelry display that doubles as art.

11. **Inspiration for More Projects:** Sometimes, one creation sparks ideas for more. Use your existing jewelry as inspiration for new projects. For instance, you might design matching pieces or variations on a theme.

12. **Document Your Creations:** Keep a journal or photo album of your jewelry-making journey. Include notes on techniques, materials, and inspiration behind each piece. It's a beautiful way to reflect on your progress.

Conclusion

Best wishes! You've begun your journey into the realm of jewelry creation by creating one-of-a-kind, handcrafted jewels out of simple materials. Now that you have the abilities to create more, you can choose to keep making things for yourself, give them as gifts to loved ones, or even consider making your hobby a business.

Making jewelry is more than simply a pastime; it's a means of expressing your uniqueness and inventiveness and realizing your ideas. The only thing stopping you as you continue experimenting with different methods, supplies, and layouts is your creativity. Your distinct perspective is reflected in every work you make, and you will develop as an artist with every new endeavor.

Thus, never stop learning, trying new things, and most importantly, never stop creating. You've only just started your jewelry journey, and there are countless options!

Made in United States
Troutdale, OR
02/21/2025